A
Kept
Woman

JULIE HAYDEN

"The thing that was sent to discredit you and destroy you has turned into the arrow to propel you to the destiny I designed for you."

~ God

CONTENTS

FORWARD

October 14, 2019

I'm sitting at the airport awaiting a flight to Rome for our 45th wedding anniversary. I was fortunate to marry the woman of my dreams and to weather through good times and bad times to get here. That's my story.

Julie's story is different. Her story takes a twist that unfortunately led to her marriage ending, her life abruptly changing, and her faith being severely tested. But the story is not a sad story of tragedy but a hopeful message of triumph. That's why I told her she must write it and many would be encouraged when they read it. What you have before you is a hope filled message that speaks honestly and transparently about her past, yet shows an ever loving Savior who walked her through the present into her glorious future!

Divorce is one of the most painful and difficult things a person will ever walk through. Perhaps second only to the loss of a child. Julie has experienced firsthand a grace that is priceless, a peace that is matchless, and a hope that is limitless. As believers, we live very idealistic lives, yet I am often amazed at how God works in our "mess". Julie's "mess" has turned into a "message" and her " grave" a "womb" of promise.

David wrote from his pain and sorrow and inspired us to keep moving past the hurt and beyond what the enemy intended to be your grave or your end. In Psalm 30:3;5a, he said, " O Lord, thou hast brought up my soul from the grave; thou hast KEPT me alive, that I should not go down to the pit...weeping may endure for a night, but joy cometh in the morning."

Julie is indeed a "kept" woman and her joy is contagious. May you be infected as well regardless of where your story takes you. Be inspired from hers and be a "carrier" of hope.

Pastor Mike Hendon

A KEPT WOMAN

JULIE HAYDEN

1 I AM A KEPT WOMAN

I am a kept woman.

I didn't choose this life. It was chosen for me.

I may not have chosen this life, but I am grateful for the One who keeps me.

He is my Keeper. He is a keeper.

It was a Tuesday. We'd just finished up a week-long family vacation. We'd had a great evening the night before talking with our sons about dreams and college plans. We had breakfast at the table together that morning. We'd all headed off to work. My husband to the church. I headed to the part-time job I'd recently started. My kids were going to their summer job volunteering at a local ministry. Just a normal Tuesday.

When I got to work, the boss pulled me aside and

asked me what we were going to do about my husband's job. I had no idea what he was talking about. My husband had just gone to work. My boss told me my husband had resigned and completed his two-week notice the day before.

I was shocked. My boss was panicked. What had he just said? Why didn't I know? He gave me the office to make any phone calls I needed.

I first called my husband's cell phone. No answer.

I called his work and asked the secretary for him. She informed me he no longer worked there and asked if she could help me. When I said I was his wife, she was stunned. "You didn't know?" "No, I don't know anything."

I phoned two pastors for prayer. One told me they would go look for him. I should stay where I was. He asked me if there was any reason my husband wouldn't tell me about quitting his job. Out of my mouth I said, "He must be having an affair."

The pastor encouraged me not to jump to any conclusions. To give him the benefit of the doubt. My husband was very faithful and trustworthy. There was no reason to think such a thing.

I had no idea why I would even think it.

But I couldn't escape it. The thoughts plagued me that morning. I was trying to work – but I couldn't concentrate. I was trying to think the best. But the pit in my stomach grew.

After about an hour my cell phone rang, and it was my husband. He told me everything was "fine" and we could talk when I got off work. But I knew I couldn't work. I was going home to find out what was happening.

He asked me to pick the kids up from their volunteer job on my way so he could talk with us all. The kids were out on a delivery and not available. So I then came home alone.

There we sat in the living room. My husband in a chair across the room. I was sitting on the couch. Places we'd sat many times. But this time, time stood still.

Within five minutes I learned that my husband had been having an 18 month internet affair. He had already filed for divorce. He had already packed his car. He had left his ministry position at the church. He would send money when he got a job. He was moving 1000 miles away. He had everything he wanted – the house was mine. The bank accounts were mine. I'd be served divorce papers any day.

There was no hope for reconciliation. No opportunities for counseling. No changing his mind. And no answers. In his words, "It's not about anything you did. This is about me."

As he spoke to me, it was like his entire

countenance changed. He suddenly became gray. It was my husband sitting there, but this was not my husband talking to me.

He told me he would go and wait to tell the kids. However, if anyone tried to stop him from leaving, he would immediately leave and I could tell them.

With that, he stood up and asked for a hug. I gave him a hug and he walked out the door. He drove out of our driveway ... for the last time.

I was STUNNED! I had no words. I had no emotions. Just shock.

What had just happened? And why did I give him a hug? It was like Judas' kiss. My best friend, my husband had just abandoned me, filed divorce, and I hugged him. What was going on?!?!?

He left our home and went to wait for our sons to return to their job site. I went separately to their work. I didn't want them alone after he spoke with them. He met and talked to them in the parking lot, telling them he was leaving and moving away. He gave them a hug. He turned and walked away from them. They walked across the parking lot to me.

I suddenly went from married with children to a single mom.

I was thrust into a world I knew nothing about. I NEVER, EVER thought we would get divorced. We

were ministry leaders. He was on staff at a church.
I ran a ministry from our house.

No marriage is perfect. Ours was not. But never in
a million years would I have believed he would
have an affair or that my marriage would end in
divorce. Never. EVER!

No one else believed me either. I phoned my dad.
I told him to sit down. He thought my grand-
mother had passed. He couldn't believe what I was
telling him. My best friend thought I was lying and
told me this was not a funny thing to joke about.
Even one of my sisters, thought I was lying. It was
so unfathomable what had just occurred.

The Senior Pastor where my husband worked,
Pastor Bob, called as soon as he learned I didn't
know about the resignation. By the time he called,
my husband was gone. He was so surprised. He
mentioned he and his wife would be by later to
pray with me.

Pastor Tony, who had been searching for my
husband, came to the house along with another
pastor. Together they sat with me, wept with me,
and prayed. They began asking what I would do, if
I had a lawyer, what were my next steps. I didn't
have any answers or any money.

In that moment, God provided! I had worked with
the area pastors for over 10 years. Pastor Tony
promised to go to every pastor in town if he had to

in order to cover the retainer for a lawyer for me. I wasn't walking alone in this. He told me, "God will provide for you." It wasn't just words – it was a promise. He told me the Lord was my Husband and He was a Defender of widows and a Father to the fatherless. I was now one and God would provide and care for me and my sons.

That day was filled with more bizarre encounters. My father quickly came to be by my side. My sons were in and out of the room as visitors came to care, came to console, and came to grieve with us.

Pastor Bob and his wife came to our house that afternoon. They were hurting. They were stunned. This was their friend and colleague. They had just been betrayed too.

"His sin is not your shame. Don't wear it."

I had felt so ashamed. How could my husband have an affair? Where had I failed as a wife? Was she better than I was? What did I do? What didn't I do? Why wasn't I enough?

Day after day. Hour after hour I would repeat Pastor Bob's words: "His sin is not your shame. Don't wear it."

As the days unfolded it would have been very easy to wear it. Like a cloak of dishonor, a coat of shame, I could put it on every morning. Put my head down. Never leave my bedroom. And never live again.

Yet I knew I could not do that. There would be a tomorrow. I had to go on. My life as I knew it had ended, but my life was not over. A new book would be written.

The hours of that first day were spent with people who loved us and who we loved. Much was in silence. There were no words. There definitely were no answers. But I was grateful to not be alone.

Before the day was over, I had called my husband's cell phone and left a message that he could turn around and come home. But I knew he would not.

I also knew my story would not be private for long. My husband and I both were in ministry. He had lied to his volunteers, team members, and staff. Before the first night ended, 75 families would be notified of what had occurred. Within two weeks, there were five public statements across the region and over 2000 people learned of the affair and impending divorce.

As that first day went on, I would remember the details of the last few months and suddenly things made sense. I felt like such a fool. I knew something wasn't right for a while, but I could never put my finger on it. When I would ask him, I would be told everything was fine. But things weren't fine. He had been distant. I had been distant.

My mom had died about 9 months before. I had been grieving and suffering some depression from that. I had health issues that started while I was caregiving for her. I was diagnosed with Meniere's Disease which is a chronic inner ear issue causing vertigo and hearing loss. I'd had two surgeries in the three months preceding him leaving. I had scaled back my ministry and career to care for my mom and my kids while my husband was pursuing his ministry.

In less than one year, I had lost my mom, my health, my hearing, my ministry, my career, and now my marriage. I had every right to just hole up in my house and never leave. But I knew that was not God's plan for me.

That Tuesday night I went to bed, but sleep was far from me. The emotions that were dammed up in the daylight became a flood that would not stop. As I lay in our bed, I wept. I wailed. I cried to the point of throwing up. There was no controlling the torrent of tears erupting inside of me.

The next morning as I got out of the shower I looked down at my left hand. I saw my wedding ring. I had always been so proud of it. It was beautiful with diamonds and rubies. I only took it off to have it repaired. I wore it all the time.

On that morning, I clearly heard the Lord tell me to

take the ring off. My husband was not returning.

I stared at my hand for a long time. Then I walked over to my jewelry box and took off the ring that had been on my hand for 21 years. There was such an indent where the ring had been. For months the imprint of the ring remained. A reminder of what had been broken and what would no longer be.

While it was hard to hear those words from the Lord, I'm so grateful for the voice of God. I'm grateful that His sheep can hear His voice. I did not have to wonder. I did not have to think about what it would be like for him to return. I knew he was not coming back. Throughout the process, I could focus on moving forward alone. I could focus on healing for me and my sons. I knew there was never going to be a possibility of restoration or reconciliation of my marriage. Only forgiveness and healing could be learned and obtained.

I began to frame my life going forward around what God had spoken to me. I didn't spend my time praying for the restoration of my marriage, I prayed for healing and for the grace to forgive. Hearing God's voice helped me each and every day. When I didn't know what to do, I would ask the Lord. So often He would bring an answer. "Call a friend." "Ask for help." "You are not alone."

I'm blown away by the ability of God to speak just what we need to hear. Often, I had to still my thoughts my will, and my emotions, but when I would seek Him, He was faithful.

He didn't speak what I wanted to hear. He spoke truth. He spoke hope. He spoke life into me and my situations.

He is my Keeper.

I thought I knew tomorrow but then I faced today
Everything I thought of has turned a different way
The world that I once knew suddenly came apart
And now I stand here holding all the pieces of my heart
I know I'll make it through the dark night of the soul
Clinging only to the Lord is the only way I know.

2 GOD PROVIDES

I wasn't spared the road of divorce. I had to face it head-first. And with thousands watching. Most divorces are very private matters. People don't find out right away. Usually it is well along before it is publicly known.

That is not the case when you are in full-time ministry.

We knew with our call that our life was public. Throughout our entire marriage of 21 years, we served in the local church and community. When we were pursuing marriage, the minister doing our premarital counseling spent much time talking about the challenges of marriage, family and ministry.

There are two sides to the coin of publicity. One side is no privacy. Everyone knows your business and many feel they have a right to know all the details because of the ministry positions. The other side of the coin was support. For so many, divorce is done in private. Our pain was very public, and with that came much concern and care. Because it was so public, so many people wanted to show their love and concern for our family. The outpouring of love was HUGE!!!

A week after my husband had left a small white envelope came in my mailbox. Inside was a green 3x5 note card with the verse, "My God will supply all your needs according to His riches in glory in Christ Jesus" and a $50 bill. No name. No return-address. As I read it, I wept.

As the days went on, God started to live out that verse in our family. Many days a week I would go to the mailbox and there would be cards or notes filled with encouragement. Oftentimes there would be checks in the mail. Gift cards. Prayers. People even went to my bank and anonymously deposited money into my account.

I didn't know what to do with all the cards I received. They were so precious to us. Words of hope. Words of life. I began to hang them on the doors and walls of our home. They were reminders that we were not alone in this journey. All together I received 77 cards in those months offering prayers, hope and encouragement.

Our church family set up meals for us. Three times

a week for six weeks dear families came and loved on my family. They loved us well with burritos, casseroles, pizzas, rainbow cake, and more. Friends brought produce from their gardens. One friend even brought toilet paper and laundry soap – it meant so much to me to know everything was covered!

Others spent time with my sons. Teaching them to drive. Taking them on driving adventures. Inviting them to the movies, trips to the beach or fun with friends.

I had begun journaling all the ways God was providing. We had a Miracle Journal for our family. We would write down significant ways God moved or provided over the years in a spiral notebook. Now it was a daily occurrence to pull it out and write down about His goodness.

We made the choice to celebrate the good. We had so much bad that was trying to consume and overwhelm us. With every journal entry, we would see God's promises fulfilled that He was going to provide.

When the fears would be overwhelming, I would pull out the Miracle Journal and read aloud all the ways God had provided. If He did it before, He could do it again.

We celebrated when we qualified for food stamps and state health insurance. We celebrated free

and reduced lunch. We thanked God for it all –
believing He is our provider.

I celebrated when my attorney did not require the
customary retainer. He had asked me to log all
financial gifts. My lawyer got to witness God
provide over $10,000 in cash or goods in that
season. He had never seen anything like it. The
faithfulness and goodness of God was so apparent
to this man!

God's provision and hand was so clear! It wasn't
just our desperate needs He was meeting, but the
desires of our souls too.

After about a month, I had been thinking about
wanting to get a new to me used bed. I didn't want
our king size bed any longer. I wanted a twin or
full-size bed – something that didn't make me feel
like someone was missing. A friend approached
me at church and asked if there was anything I
needed. I mentioned I was wanting to get a bed.
She told me to meet her at the furniture store that
week.

I'll never forget going into that store to buy a
mattress. I laid on the beds and was struck with
laughter and amazement. What a crazy thing I was
getting to do!?!!?! I'm sure the salesperson
thought I was insane.

Other friends heard that someone had purchased a
mattress for me, and they purchased a new bed

frame. Friends came and redecorated my room. My bible study group made me a quilt. God was giving me a new bedroom.

When I was preparing to paint my bedroom, many friends came and wrote Bible verses on the walls. I wanted to be surrounded in the Word of God. They prayed and then wrote their prayers on the bedroom walls. One scripture kept coming to mind for me. I put it on my ceiling in yellow marker. It still bleeds through the paint to this day.

Psalm 121

I will lift up my eyes to the hills- From whence comes my help?

My help come from the LORD, Who made heaven and earth.

He will not allow your foot to be moved; He who keeps you will not slumber

Behold, He who keeps Israel shall neither slumber nor sleep.

The LORD is your KEEPER; the LORD is your shade at your right hand.

The sun shall not strike you by day, nor the moon by night.

The LORD shall preserve you from all evil;

He shall preserve your soul.

The LORD shall preserve your going out and your coming in from this time forth, and even forevermore.

This Psalm has become an anthem for me over the last seven years. The LORD is my Keeper. He is my Life Preserver. He will not allow me to be moved! He holds all things together and doesn't stop! I can rest, because He never sleeps or slumbers on my behalf.

God has continually provided. Every bill was paid. Every need was met. My kids were provided for. They were able to continue with the clubs and music lessons they had been taking. God continued to provide through His body.

All the while I was looking for a fulltime job to support my family. At the time of the separation I made less than $400 a month. After about three months, I was hired by a law firm. It was the perfect position for my family.

Just like the manna in the wilderness, the week I received my new job, the checks in the mail stopped. It was like Someone had shut off the faucet. God was now providing in a new way. I was grateful for however He would provide.

God wanted me to know that He still was with us and not leaving us. The week my divorce was final three families gave us $500 gifts. WOW! In the Bible the number five represents Grace. It was like

God was shouting, "GRACE, GRACE, GRACE" over our family.

God's word instructs us in Malachi 3:10 *"Bring all the tithes into the storehouse, that there may be food in My house, and try Me now in this," says the LORD of hosts, "If I will not open for you the windows heaven and pour out for you such blessing that there will not be room enough to receive it. And I will rebuke the devourer for your sakes, so that he will not destroy the fruit of your ground, nor shall the vine fail to bear fruit for you in the field," says the LORD of hosts. "*

I'm grateful my parents instilled in me the importance of tithing. Throughout this trial I saw God be faithful to His word. My kids saw God's promise fulfilled to open the windows of heaven and pour out blessings we couldn't contain.

Despite the financial hardship in faced, we continued to tithe to our local church. We daily watched the Lord rebuke the enemy of our souls off our finances. God provided what we needed. We always had enough when we would put Him first and give our first to Him.

Over and over again, we were blessed. At one point during the initial days we had so much produce and food coming we couldn't eat it fast enough. One of my coworkers was asking how we were doing and if we had enough meat. In that moment, I realized her family didn't have what they needed. For the next few months, not only did God provide for us, but God provided for this dear family with the overflow. God even allowed us to share with hungry in our time of need. There was ALWAYS ENOUGH!

God continually met every need with abundance. At one point, I realized that we needed to prepare for the future. We had so much food that could be stored for a future time if we had a freezer. I began to ask for a freezer. God not only provided one freezer – He provided two! Everywhere we turned, God was pouring out in abundance and extravagance.

Over the last seven years, I haven't had unlimited cash supply. I haven't built a nest egg. I have still had to go to work every day. But I have seen God provide everything we had need of. I've seen Him provide for my sons to graduate college with minimal debt. I was able to finish my college degree debt free. We've purchased three cars without payments. We were given two cars. God has met every need.

He is Faithful to rebuke the devourer on our behalf. Our cars lasted so much longer than they should have. God has stretched our little to be enough. I've seen Him provide - day in and day out. Not usually early, but always an on-time God. We did not lack what we truly needed.

At one point, I was very concerned about my sons

feeling like they were poor. What I realized was that in a time when the world would see us below the poverty level, we never felt richer. Our lives were enriched by seeing the faithfulness of God demonstrated by the body of Christ. It wasn't any one person. It wasn't even the church as a whole. It was individual members of the body of Christ each being obedient to what God had asked of them. We are rich indeed!

Obey the Lord. Bring in your whole tithes and offering. Try the Lord in this! God is faithful. He truly gave seed to this sower.

He is my Keeper!

3 THE ROAD CALLED FORGIVENESS

Shortly after the divorce was final, I received a call from my ex-husband. He had remarried. It was like a nail being driven into the casket of my marriage. In that moment, I knew that if God could provide financially for us, I could trust God could provide emotionally for us too. He would give me the grace to forgive and provide the healing we all needed.

Forgiveness is a choice. It isn't a feeling. It is a determination. It is a resolve.

The week my husband left I made the decision I would choose to forgive. I didn't know how I would do it, but I determined that somehow, with God's grace, I would.

At first it was a moment by moment occurrence. Everything in my life had turned upside down. I was mad. I was angry. I was frustrated and bewildered. I didn't have any answers. I just had hurt.

I knew it would be easy to grow in bitterness if I wasn't proactive in forgiveness. Forgiveness was a posture I would take, a position I would hold, and a progression I would walk out.

As I sat in my living room in the days immediately following the separation, I resolved to forgive. I determined I would forgive.

Joyce Meyer states that unforgiveness is like drinking poison and expecting the other person to die. Forgiveness was something I needed for myself even more than it was needed for my husband. I could not allow the root of bitterness to grow in me. It would eat me alive.

When I would come face to face with situations that were direct results of the divorce, I would speak out loud, "I choose to forgive." Honestly, many times I didn't believe the words. Yet, I knew by faith it was working something in me where one day I would be able to not just voice the words but truly, with my whole being, embrace that forgiveness and release it all to God.

Forgiveness is not forgetting. Nothing could change what had occurred. The circumstances of our divorce would never change. They were just facts.

However, forgiveness was releasing the desire for the other person to pay for their actions. It was removing me from the place of God and judge in his life, allowing God to move in. It was praying for them not for judgment, but for mercy and grace. It was blessing my enemies and wishing them well.

At first, I had moment by moment reminders of how my life was different.

My career path was closed. So, I'd whisper, "I choose to forgive."

I was a single parent. Again, I'd tell myself, "I choose to forgive."

I had the stress of balancing my home, work, and life. "I choose to forgive."

So many things I'd never done before that I suddenly had to take the lead. "I choose to forgive."

I was continually faced with opportunities to burn with anger. So, over and over I'd whisper - and even shout, "I choose to forgive!"

As time went on, God began to move in my ex-husband's life. I'm grateful for the amazing work God has done. After nine months, he reached out to me and asked my forgiveness for the situations regarding our divorce. At that time, I was able to say I forgive you because I had lots of practice in the months before.

Still to this day there are situations that trigger moments where I feel like this is all so unfair. I feel like I should not have had to deal with this pain. I can start to blame, but God gently reminds me "choose to forgive."

Matthew 18:21-35 (ESV)
The Parable of the Unforgiving Servant
21 Then Peter came up and said to him, "Lord, how often will my brother sin against me, and I forgive him? As many as seven times?" 22 Jesus said to him, "I do not say to you seven times, but seventy-seven times.

23 "Therefore the kingdom of heaven may be compared to a king who wished to settle accounts with his servants. 24 When he began to settle, one was brought to him who owed him ten thousand talents. 25 And since he could not pay, his master ordered him to be sold, with his wife and children and all that he had, and payment to be made. 26 So the servant fell on his knees, imploring him, 'Have patience with me, and I will pay you everything.' 27 And out of pity for him, the master of that servant released him and forgave him the debt. 28 But when that same servant went out, he found one of his fellow servants who owed him a hundred denarii, and seizing him, he began to choke him, saying, 'Pay what you owe.' 29 So his fellow servant fell down and pleaded with him, 'Have patience with me, and I will pay you.' 30 He refused and went and put him in prison until he

*should pay the debt. 31 When his fellow servants
saw what had taken place, they were greatly
distressed, and they went and reported to their
master all that had taken place. 32 Then his master
summoned him and said to him, 'You wicked
servant! I forgave you all that debt because you
pleaded with me. 33 And should not you have had
mercy on your fellow servant, as I had mercy on
you?'34 And in anger his master delivered him to the
jailers, until he should pay all his debt. 35 So also my
heavenly Father will do to every one of you, if you
do not forgive your brother from your heart."*

The Lord has forgiven each one of us so much.
How can we not forgive those in our lives? Jesus
instructed that we don't just forgive one time and
are done. But seventy times seven. It is a perpetual
forgiveness. It is an ongoing process. We must
choose to forgive and choose to continually
forgive. With each reminder we choose to forgive.

If we do not choose to forgive, we are bound up
and handed over to the jailers of our soul!
Unforgiveness will torment you day and night.
Your unforgiveness will destroy your life and your
health. Your bitterness from unforgiveness will not
only defile you. It will defile all you come in
contact with.

 Your protection and peace is found in learning to
forgive. Forgive as you have been forgiven. Deeply.
From the heart. With full assurance in a merciful

God.

His grace is enough even for this! His grace to forgive is a gift we can receive. Open your heart. Choose to forgive. Release the other person and free yourself!

God, give us the grace to forgive!

Come be our Keeper!

4 A TIME TO MOURN

Ecclesiastes 3 states that there is a time and season for everything. There is a time to weep and a time to laugh. A time to mourn and a time to dance.

We grieve because we loved. Grief is a constant reminder of the losses we have experienced.

Grief is no respecter of persons. It will strike at the most inopportune times.

October 2011 through December 2012 was an intense time of loss for me. In eighteen months, I lost my health, my hearing, my mom, my marriage, my ministry, my career path, my dreams, my future and my financial security. It wasn't just one loss, but compiled losses that led me to the most sorrowful time of my life.

Just as I was rebuilding my life after my mother's death, the bottom dropped out on my family. I had no idea what was going on. I had been lost in my grief and missed the warning signs all around. Looking back, I can now see so much. But in the moment, I was swirling in the downward spiral of grief.

Elizabeth Kubler-Ross wrote and taught extensively on the Five Stages of Grief Cycle. The Five Stages are Denial, Anger, Bargaining, Depression, and Acceptance. While we grieve, we can go through each stage, sometimes multiple times, on our way to acceptance and moving forward.

With my mom we knew her death was imminent. We had over six years of preparing for the end. When my mom passed away, my first reaction was a relief. She had been ill for so long. She was now out of her misery and with the Lord. Yet, as time went by, I realized how much I missed her. Even things that frustrated me over the last years of her life, were suddenly missed. When all the dust had settled and I no longer was caring for her, the reality and finality of her death began to sink in.

However, nothing prepared me for the sudden and raw pain of the July 3, 2012. When trauma of any sort hits, the feelings intensify. The lack of control. The fears that would plague my mind. The never knowing what might be around the corner.

I never used to worry or stress about sudden changes. I was a planner. Most of my life was lived with some foreknowledge. However not that day!

Suddenly every dream, every plan, every security was ripped out with one sudden goodbye.

Shocked. Stunned. Devastated. I have never felt so awestruck and dumbfounded. I couldn't even process what was happening. There were no words. It was like I was living someone else's life for those first few days.

And the pain. I have never felt such pain. It would

28

come in waves. It would be overwhelming. One moment I would be in stunned silence. The next moment I was whimpering. At other times guttural groans with tears and screams would come. Often, I would cry until I threw up. When I was alone and the tears could come, there was no stopping it.

Because of the suddenness and shock, every situation outside of my control would set off sudden shock waves of anger, sadness, or fear. Since I had lacked any control in my divorce, I tried to manage my life in the days immediately surrounding the abandonment with careful planning. I did not like surprises. I did not like the unknown – whether good or bad.

Still that fear of the unknown can be paralyzing. It is hard to move forward in your life when you want to control everything. In moving forward, I had to take risks which for many would not be overwhelming. To live you must risk. I'm **_choosing_** to live again.

I'm grateful that the counselors encouraged me to grieve. They encouraged me to feel all the emotions. Feel the pain. Feel the anger. Feel the betrayal. Feel the loss. No one told me to hold it together. They gave me permission to feel and permission to cry.

Most days I could hold it together. I began working and for those eight hours I found peace as my mind was occupied. But when I would get in the car to drive home, the weight would sometimes overtake me.

I created a crying chair in my house. I knew when I sat in that chair, I was safe and could feel any emotion. I would often get dinner made and get the kids situated for the evening. Then, I would take a few minutes, go in my room and close the door. I'd sit in the chair and breath. I'd pray and ask God to help me let this go. And then I'd give myself permission to cry.

I would try to hold it together during the day. Try to hold it together and be strong for my family. Be strong for those that were watching. But in my crying chair it was just me and God. And He was not afraid of my emotions. He never told me to pull it together. He just would whisper "I AM here. I AM with you. You are OK. It's OK to cry."

I found that grace at my church too. Immediately after the separation, I returned to our sending church. I needed a safe place for my kids and I to heal. I found it in Family Bible Church.

I had always served on Sunday morning. It was more normal for me to serve than to sit. I'm grateful for pastors who didn't shun me but blessed me to do whatever I was able from my former normal life. I had been asked if I wanted to serve on a worship team just a few weeks after the separation. It was a great place of connection, love and support for me.

Sundays were my hardest days of the week. So much of church is geared to couples and families. I felt like such an outsider. I would see the wives reach over and grab the hands of their husbands in worship and my heart would just break.

Each week I would serve on our worship team. There were weeks I couldn't finish the music sets. Most weeks it was a good distraction. Usually after we finished, I would go find an empty classroom and cry for a bit. I had the best pastor. He and his wife would give me some time. If I didn't come into the sanctuary within 10-15 minutes, they would come check on me. They never told me to stop crying or to pull it together. They would only ask if I needed anything: prayer, water, or someone to just sit and cry with me. I'm so grateful for these dear friends.

"I never knew you lived so close to the floor,

But every time I am bowed down,

Crushed by this weight of grief,

I feel your hand on my head,

Your breath on my cheek,

Your tears on my neck.

You never tell me to pull myself together,

To stem the flow of many years.

You simply stay by my side

For as long as it takes,

So close to the floor." Sheila Walsh, *Honestly*

As time went on, God began to heal and my grieving lessened. In DivorceCare I learned that the indicators of improvement are measured by the intensity, duration, and frequency of the grief. Over time, I could weep without feeling out of control. At first it seemed like I was always crying. That it would never stop. Then daily. I remember celebrating when I realized I hadn't cried for more than one day. The intensity, duration and frequency began to be my measuring stick. If I could see progress in any area, I knew I was moving forward.

As time went on, I began to realize the magnitude of my loss. I knew I had lost my future. The dreams I had for our life together were over. We wouldn't be grandparents together. We wouldn't grow old together. The trips we planned would never happen. The security I found in knowing I would not be alone or die alone were all ripped from me.

My present was radically different. I grieved the loss of my career and ministry path. I watched a ministry I had built for 12 years decay and die. I closed the book on so many unfinished chapters of my life.

Yet, the most shocking loss to me was the loss of my past. Because my husband's actions impacted so many people, they all experienced pain as well when reminded about him. To my friends who knew him, I also lost my past. None of my friends could bear to hear any stories from my married life. Suddenly even the good times were removed from peoples' memories. They could not withstand the trauma of sorting through it. Along with my present and future, my past had died that day.

As you grieve, ask God to reveal what are the losses you are grieving. Take time to feel them and let God heal them. Don't try to rush through your grief. Grief is not on your timetable. Let God complete the work in you.

Surround yourself with people who will encourage you

and who will also just cry with you. As you are able, begin to engage in the lives of others again. Allow yourself to celebrate their joys and walk with them. Don't forget in your pain to remember to be a friend to your friends. It will help you as well to look beyond yourself and will bring joy back to your life again.

With the comfort you have received from the Lord, you will eventually be able to comfort others. I have so much more empathy for those going through death, divorce or loss because of what I have lost. I never knew what it was like. I made critical judgments out of my ignorance before walking this journey. Now I know the pain. And I know the need to just be loved in the process.

The Lord is your Keeper!

Alone

He walked her home.

He finished right by her side.

He was there every step; every painful step.

My dad, my hero.

But who will be there to walk me home?

I know Who will be on the other side.

But this thing called life seems scary.

It's lonely. I am alone.

Sure, friends are there when I need them most.

But in the day to day, the ups and downs, I am alone.

I think my greatest fear is dying alone.

Yet implied in that is living alone.

I don't know which is worse-

To walk every day alone and have someone there at the critical times.

Or to have those with you every day but just missing the very last.

A KEPT WOMAN

Yeah, maybe this life alone is the worst.

We were made to walk in community, live in community, be community.

So why are we all so divided.

Why are we all so busy, we don't have time for one another.

Time to just be.

I miss being in a room with a friend or my spouse and not having to say anything.

Just comfortable being together.

Now I'm so longing for connection and communication that the time is filled with words...

Sometimes meaningless, trivial words.

Where is that person to ask me how my day was and care enough to listen to the answer?

Where is that person that I can ask the same of?

Where is that person that will be here in the "ugly of life" and whisper it will be ok?

Why am I feeling so alone?

(Thoughts from 2013)

5 ONE IS A WHOLE NUMBER

I think loneliness is the most devastating and overwhelming feelings of being single.

That first night I remember trying to go to bed. The bed was so large. The bed was so empty. Just lying there with the empty space next to me screamed "YOU ARE ALONE".

All day, I had been surrounded by people. My dad came over to be with us. A few pastors came by to pray and sit in shock with us. Our best couple friends had me and my sons over for dinner – making sure we ate and weren't alone.

That first day I really only experienced shock. It was like a bad made for TV movie. But unfortunately, it was real and not make believe.

No answers. No understanding. No hope of restoration. Only devastation.

I never dreamed I would be faced with the challenges of that day. I never dreamed I would be divorced. I never dreamed I would be alone.

When the people were around, I was just in shock. I had very few words. I had no emotions. I had no understanding.

But when I was faced with the empty bed, suddenly I couldn't hold back the pain. The tears. The grief. The fear. The disbelief. The anger. The vomiting.

Alone. No hope for restoration. No hope for return. He was gone and I was alone.

God never created us to be alone. Even in the garden, God spoke to Adam that it was not good that he was alone. So He created woman.

Fundamentally there is something within each of us that desires to not be alone. Whether you are single by choice or circumstances, we were made for community. We were made for fellowship with God and others.

Since the time I was 21, I was always a couple. I didn't know how to be single. I didn't know how to be alone.

Over my 21 years of marriage, 95% of my friends were couples. I loved my single friends, but I didn't understand their world or their struggles. My world was couples and families.

Over 95% of all pastors are married. Only 5% of all evangelical pastors are single and even more surprising only 2% of evangelical lead/senior pastors are single. The church speaks often about families and couples. Sundays would be such a challenge. I suddenly didn't fit into the typical pastor's sermon illustration. My grid for life had changed. My world had shifted.

I suddenly was aware of couples EVERYWHERE! I'd walk in the room and the wives would subconsciously grab their husband's arms or hands. I was an "other" in the circle of friends. Suddenly, I didn't know my place in the world.

All the while I didn't know anything of the new world of single adult. Over the course of two years, my friend grid began to change. I began to realize I had a lot more in common with the singles in my church. My demographic had changed and everything in my life started to align.

One hard consequence of that was the lack of male conversation. Males think and talk differently than females. I missed those conversations. I was very grateful to the few female friends that were not threatened by my singleness and would allow their husbands to talk with me when I needed male advice.

God created us male and female for a reason. In families and in churches, we need both voices to be heard to complete the image of God. There was a reason God said that it was not good for man to be alone in the Garden.

Sometimes it is hard to not have that other person who is looking out for you. I often see how spouses defend and support each other. There is great strength found in knowing someone else has your back and is your cheerleader, pushing you on.

As a single this can be such a challenge. I must constantly remind myself that the Lord is my Husband. He is my defender and my keeper. He is my encourager. He is my shield from the arrows of the outside world that would pierce my heart through. He is my healer.

Often, I wish that I had that husband here - live and in person. A friend would refer to this as "Jesus with skin on." While we can know that He is our comfort, sometimes we just long for a real hug.

In the first year, there was a time the Lord allowed me to have that "Jesus with skin on" hug. I remember the Saturday so well. I was so broken. I was so hurt. I had been sitting in my crying chair, trying to pull myself together. I remember praying, "God I just need to know You are here."

The next morning as I was preparing to lead worship the guitar player came up to me. Without warning, he wrapped his arms around me and he didn't let go! Normally for single girls, married men will only give you a side hug at best. But this was a full-on bear hug, and he held on for dear life. In that moment, God hugged me through a faithful, willing, humble man.

Being single you are alone – but you don't have to be lonely. The Bible teaches that He sets the solitary in families. (Psalm 68:6) You can be amidst a crowd of people and be lonely. Lonely is an inward feeling.

It has taken years to distinguish between alone and lonely. Introverts can like being alone, yet not feel lonely at all. Alone is simply defined as having no one else present. While lonely is defined by emotions. Loneliness is feeling sad because one has no friends or company. There is a sorrow attached with loneliness.

Alone is not the problem – loneliness is.

How do we overcome loneliness? I found over the years I needed to be strategic about when and who I place around myself. In certain situations, being with people can make me more discontent with the life I now lead. I would weigh whether the end result of the event or gathering was worth the enjoyment of the moment. I would love every gathering I attended, but going home to the empty house with no one to share it with was often brutal. Know yourself! Know your circumstances.

As singles we must really guard our hearts. No one else will do it for you. You must get to know yourself. Know when you need time with others and when you need time with God. He is the best healer. He is the friend that is closer than a brother. He is the One who lifts your head. He is your Husband and strength.

We often try to fill the voids with others that only He can fill. Only He has the words of life. He can speak through others, but many times we seek others to try to bypass Him.

In the book *Finding Contentment*, Neil Clark Warren states that we will never know true contentment until we are truly authentic. We must find our authentic identity in Christ alone. He is our Source. He created us and knows us better than anyone else. We must seek Him to write His new identity on our hearts. Until He speaks it, we will walk in darkness and flounder. We will never be content. We will never be whole. We will be lonely.

Yet when He writes His story on our hearts, we become alive! We have a purpose. We have a hope. We have an identity. We are no longer just an "other." We are more than enough. We are filled with HOPE!

Jeremiah 29:11 states that He knows the plans He has for us to give us a future and a hope. We do not need to flounder. We only need to seek Him with all of our hearts. He longs to be found by us and fill the voids in our life.

One is a whole number. It is not a less than position. It is whole. It is more than enough. If God has allowed you to be single in this season, then He has a plan to use even your singleness for His glory and good.

Paul mentioned how he was glad that he was single. It allowed him to do things that those that have families could not. He could be single minded for the work of the Lord.

In my singleness I have found that I have opportunities that I never would have had if I had remained married. I did not wish for my singleness, but God is bringing about amazing new things as I yield to His plan in this time. I do not have to think about what my husband would want. Instead, I only think about what God would want.

My time is my own. I am free to make decisions about how I spend my time that I never would be able to do if I was not single. I am free to serve. I am free to go to dinner with a hurting friend. I have freedom to focus on the Lord.

Nothing holds me back. I could relocate anywhere. I could move around the world! I can go wherever He leads me.

In his book, *Emotionally Healthy Leader*, Peter Scazzero states that our primary witness to the world is our marriage or our singleness. In marriage, we show the beauty of how Christ loved the church and gave His life for it. In our singleness, we show the broadness of His great love for all.

As a single, we are not devoted just to one person. We are given the freedom to love well all who come into our lives. There is a broadness to our love and a broadness to our capacity to love. We learn to pour it out to the world, not just our home.

Unique challenges face singles. We do have to remember that we must care for ourselves and our homes. No one else is there to do it for us. There are still groceries to buy, laundry to wash and a house to clean that only we are responsible for. However, there is great joy that can come as we celebrate all that we are enabled to do in our singleness.

When we only focus on our aloneness and loneliness, we miss the joys of singlehood. We must continually remind ourselves that the Lord has allowed this season in our lives and we have been given a great privilege to serve Him wholly and completely.

6 SEX AND THE SINGLE

Often when we are not content in our singleness, we will look for love in all the wrong places. We try to fill our voids with others. We long for the aches to go away, but if we aren't careful we wind up in bigger messes.

I believe that dating too soon is the number one downfall of most newly single adults. They run to the first person that shows attention and they give themselves away, body and soul, to their own hurt. They think they have found love, but all they have done is put a band-aid on an infected wound. The wounds continue to spread infection and ooze on all they come in contact with. Our wounds must be cleaned out and healed. Without healing, we will add to our pain, rejection, and loneliness.

Sex is not the answer. I'm shocked at the number of Godly, Christian men and women, who when faced with singleness, find themselves throwing out their convictions and throwing themselves into each other's beds. You will not be healed in sin. Sin can never satisfy. Only God can fill those longings.

For years I searched for Godly information about what to do with my sexuality as a single. I asked single friends. I scanned the internet. I would search the scriptures. Other than don't fornicate, don't commit adultery, be modest, and don't use porn, there were no real answers to the questions I was asking.

What would God have us do with our sexual desires?

Why did He create us with these desires and then not allow them to be fulfilled?

Is it wrong to have a desire?

What is lust?

What about masturbation?

How far is too far?

I felt like a teenager again on this quest for information. Yet, as a teenager, I was never sexually active. Having been active, your body, soul and spirit long for true intimacy with a person here on earth.

So, what do you do with these desires?

About a year after I was divorced, I came face to face with these questions. Up until that point, I had been so overwhelmed in just the day to day struggles of surviving that I had not given my sexuality much thought. But while sitting in a Divorcecare class, one brave woman asked the questions: "What do I do with my desire for sex? Is it wrong to have self-gratification?"

I was the leader of the class and I had no answers. I only had more questions. Up until that point I had never even thought seriously about these issues.

In response to that brave woman, I spoke what I did know clearly from Scripture:

Adultery is sin and never permitted. You should not sleep with or date a married man/woman.

Fornication is sin. Any sex outside of the covenant of marriage as God intended it is off limits. Both heterosexual and homosexual acts are sin.

The use of pornography or fantasy is wrong. As a man thinks in his heart, so is he. If a man lusts after a woman, he has already committed adultery with her. For women I think fantasy is very dangerous. Dreaming about what it would be like to be with someone is lust. It is sin. Period.

So what do we do with the urges and desires?

It is ignorant to not address them. It is foolish to think that because you are a believer, you will never have a sexual thought or you will never have a desire.

Our bodies are created in the image of God. We were created to desire intimacy with others and with God. We were created to have biological (body), emotional (soul), and spiritual components.

In true spiritual intimacy, all three, body, soul and spirit, are affected. Sex was never meant to be cheapened to just a physical act. It was meant to be all encompassing and all consuming. God designed sexual intimacy within marriage to join and bind two people together so tightly that nothing could separate them.

That is why sexual encounters outside of the covenant of marriage are so dangerous! We are giving ourselves away, body, soul and spirit, to people who have no commitment to us. Part of us is given away with each experience. We lose a part of ourselves in the tearing away and broken covenant.

God meant for sex to bond people together. It is the super glue that is meant to help hold the marriage together. Sex inside of marriage is extremely important. It wasn't meant to just be a fun bonus – it was intended to be a sign of the covenant. It wasn't supposed to be treated lightly – the marriage bed was to be pure and undefiled for a reason. When we have sex outside of marriage, we cheapen the intention of God and we lessen our covenant.

Song of Solomon 8:4 warns us to not awake or arouse love before it's time. As singles, we need to guard our purity. Purity in our mind, body, soul and spirit. We are to live a pure life before the Lord and before the world. If we allow sexual sin in our lives, it will hinder our intimacy with the Lord. Sin always separates us from God.

It's easy to know what is sin where the Bible is clear. But what about the areas that the Bible is not as clear? I grew up in a church that would say, "we speak where the Bible speaks and we are silent where the Bible is silent." What does the Bible have to say about single sexuality, masturbation, sexual desires and urges?

The questions began a quest for information and understanding. As I studied, prayed, read anything I could get my hands on, and sought the Lord, He began to speak to me about this subject of single sexuality. Over time my questions began to change. I was no longer asking if masturbation is a sin or how far is too far. God was having me examine my own heart.   What was fueling the passions in me? Why was I desiring sex in the first place? Where would the urges or desires lead me if acted upon?

I began to see this was all a matter of motives. I

discovered that the key to knowing what to do with sexual urges and desires was found in discovering what was fueling them. Knowing why you are having the desires or urges can lead you to practical solutions.

If you are single and experiencing sexual desires, I would encourage you to ask yourself these questions:

1. Is this a biological need?

For men and women there are physiological needs God placed in our bodies. Find out is this an actual biological need. Speaking to the women, God created our bodies to release hormones at different times throughout our monthly cycles. Get to know your hormones. Get to know your cycles. Is there a hormonal release occurring in your body? Are you ovulating? Is it time for your period? As a female, God created your body to desire sex at your most fertile times. Just learning to know your body can bring great comfort. To know "this too shall pass" can be all that you need!

During times where our biological needs are high, limit stimulus that would accentuate desire for sex. Watch what you are watching on TV. Be careful the discussions you entertain. Guard your mind and your heart. What you meditate on will dominate.

An additional suggestion that was given to me was learning to have proper touch. Our skin is our largest organ. We need physical connection, but it doesn't need to be sexual. Give and receive appropriate hugs. Learn healthy, appropriate touch.

2. Is this an emotional need?

Are you longing to have a good heart to heart conversation with someone who gets you? Are you lonely? Do you feel hurt or discouraged? Is it a need a friend could meet?

Schedule a dinner with a good friend. Pour out your heart to them. Listen. Laugh. Allow their words to touch your soul.

Find things that feed your soul. Have that extra cup of coffee with a friend. Rest.

Other people aren't mind readers. Reach out. Make that call. Find a friend that you can call and just say I need to talk today. Be honest. Be real. Allow yourself to heal and be restored.

3. Is this a spiritual need?

In sex there can be such a deep intimacy built with your partner. As a single, that level of intimacy can only be found with the Lord. Often, we will look for it in others. However, sin will never satisfy. Only God can satisfy the true longings of our heart. True communion is only found in the Lord.

Take extra time in worship and prayer. Get alone with God and allow Him to speak into the very depths of your being. Ask Him to come and fill those voided areas of your life. Seek to know Him more and more.

His word promises us that He is a Husband to the widow. He is the One we can cry out to – even about the most intimate details of our lives. And He is the One who can fill each of these voids.

Once you know what the need is in your life, you can begin to find the tools to deal with it. Each type of need is met in different ways. Learn yourself! It is a journey of self-awareness.

Guard yourself when you are in times of temptation. Be careful what you expose yourself to. Watch what you are watching! Pay attention to what you are filling your mind with. Psalm 119:9 states that we can stay pure by staying obedient to God's Word.

If you struggle with sexual sin and lust, I would recommend the book *Eyes of Honor* by Jonathan Welton. Knowing our identity in Christ is vital to

our freedom in these areas.   Take extra time in the
Word and prayer. Get to know who God says you
are.

Even in our aloneness and sexuality, the Lord is our
Keeper.

*"Do not fear, for you will not be ashamed;
Neither be disgraced, for you will not be put
to shame; For you will forget the shame of
your youth and will not remember the
reproach of your widowhood anymore. For
your Maker is your husband, the LORD of
hosts is His name; and your Redeemer is the
Holy One of Israel; He is called the God of
the whole earth. For the LORD has called
you like a woman forsaken and grieved in
spirit, like a youthful wife when you were
refused," says your God. "For a mere
moment I have forsaken you, but with great
mercies I will gather you. With a little wrath
I hid my face from you for a moment; But
with everlasting kindness I will have mercy
on you," says the LORD your Redeemer.*
Isaiah 54

7 HOPE FOR THOSE THAT HURT

Shame. Fear. Rejection…. This was the Trifecta of Hurt for me.

My pastor knew that shame would try to come heavy on me. That first day, he spoke, "His sin is not your shame. Don't wear it."

Often times when we are in the midst of a devastating situation we wrap ourselves in the shame, hurt and disappointment of the events. We think we have to wear it – like a scarlet letter. I was so burdened by the words divorce, affair, and betrayed. As you wear the words, they sow seeds into your heart and produce a crop of hurt and devastation.

We need to root out all the shame and rejection in our lives. We need to pluck it out and not let it seed itself in our hearts. It is such an infectious weed that seeks to overtake and destroy the garden of God's goodness.

Over and over I would repeat the words of Psalm 27:14 "I WILL SEE the Goodness of the Lord in the Land of the Living." I had to continually speak that this was not my end. This was not God's best for me. This was not God's plan for me. He had something so much greater. I WOULD see it with my very own eyes.

The shame and rejection will lead to a depression that will smother all life from you. It will make you ineffective for living. It will seem better to hide than to come out and live.

You may have been betrayed. You may have been abandoned. You may have been rejected. But it is not who you are. It is just something that happened to you. Don't internalize it! Don't let it be the core of who you are.

You are a child of God. You are a son or daughter of the Most High. You are filled with every good thing. He loads you down with benefits. He loves you. He delights in you. He smiles over you.

God has not and will not reject you.

God has not and will not abandon you.

God has not and will not condemn you.

The voice of condemnation is the voice of the accuser of the brethren. The enemy longs to get you to believe his lies over God's truth. You must renounce the lies. Reject what he is whispering over you.

Then grab hold of the truths from God's word and speak them over your life. Neil Anderson in his book, *Victory Over the Darkness*, has a great list of all the things you are in Christ. Read it over yourself out loud. Declare who God says you are.

You are the apple of His eye.

You are chosen

You are not abandoned

You are not forsaken.

You are loved with an everlasting love.

You are a royal priesthood.

You are holy.

You are the righteousness of God in Christ Jesus.

You are sealed with the Holy Spirit.

You are an ambassador for Christ.

You are mighty through God to pull down strongholds.

And the list goes on....

Take time to rise up in who you are and reject the lies, shame and rejection the enemy would want to trap you in. You can be free and rise above.

Choose to walk free from fear. Fear will paralyze you and keep you trapped in worry and doubt. What if this happens? What if that happens? Don't live your life in the "what if". Live in the goodness of God. God is faithful to be trusted with your future.

Jesus is our Peace and brings peace into the most harried places of our lives. He can calm the storms within and around us with just a whisper and a word. Let Him speak His destiny over you. He has a glorious future planned for you filled with HOPE!

Choose to live again. Don't allow the devastation of the moment to be the end of your life. The rest of your life is ahead of you and you get the privilege of stepping into it. If there are sins in your life, repent and get right with God. Then step into the NEW He has for you.

He has a wonderful, beautiful life ahead of you.

"'Enlarge the place of your tent, and let them stretch out the curtains of your dwellings; Do not spare; Lengthen your cords, and strengthen your stakes. For you shall expand to the right and to the left, and your descendants will inherit the nations, and make the desolate cities inhabited. Do not fear for you will not be ashamed; Neither be disgraced for you will not be put to shame; for you will forget the shame of your youth and will not remember the reproach of your widowhood anymore. For your Maker is your husband, the LORD of hosts is His

name; and your Redeemer is the Holy One of Israel;
He is called the God of the whole earth. For the
LORD has called you like a woman forsaken and
grieved in spirit, like a youthful wife when you were
refused,' says your God. 'For a mere moment I have
forsaken you, but with great mercies I will gather
you. With a little wrath I hid MY face from you for
a moment; but with everlasting kindness I will have
mercy on you, ' Says the LORD, your Redeemer."
Isaiah 54:2-8

This is not your end. This is only the beginning of
the new life that God has for you. He is your
Husband. He has formed you. He is with you.

God will come and heal your heart. He will gather
all the fragments of your life and make you whole
again. Then He is leading you to an enlarged place.
This is not the end.

Commit to daily Bible study and prayer. You must
have your mind continually renewed through the
Word of God. Daily Bible reading washes our mind
with truth. It lets us know the baseline for our
lives. In prayer, we are given the opportunity to
connect with God on a heart to heart level. We can
pour out our joys, our hurts and our struggles
knowing that He hears us and cares for us. He
never tires of hearing our cries and He comes and
wipes every tear away. When we don't even know
how to pray, the Holy Spirit can pray through us,
even in our groans, cries and tears.

Surround yourself with Godly friends who will pray for you, speak truth to you, hold you accountable, and cheer you on to your destiny! In our darkest times, our friends can speak words of hope over us. They can see what we cannot and can declare it over us.

Take time to dream again with God. Get a fresh vision for your life! God still has good plans for your life and longs to give you hope for your future. (Jeremiah 29:11) Without a vision, we will perish in the wilderness of survival instead of seeing our new promised land.

Stay connected to your church family. Now more than ever you need the body of Christ! This is not a time to isolate. This is a time to allow your church to pray for you, to encourage you, and to love you back to life. Get into the presence of God and allow His anointing to break every yoke!

Be careful of your self-talk. We are constantly talking to ourselves. Psychologists say that you believe what you say to yourself more than what others say to you or about you. What we rehearse in our mind has great impact on our destiny. Choose to take every thought captive to the obedience of Christ. Make sure that the thoughts you are thinking about reflect His plans for you. Begin by speaking truth and life over yourself moment by moment. Instead of rehearsing the hurts, begin declaring the new future God has in store for you. Declare your destiny!

For years I thought that my divorce would define me and keep me from ever being back in ministry again. One day I was talking with my pastor and he asked me, "Do you believe your divorce disqualified you for ministry?" I was so taken back. I was speechless! I didn't know how to answer his question.

For five years I would have said yes. I thought that I could never be of use to the body of Christ because I was divorced. I thought I was unlovable, not valuable. I thought I was a second-class Christian. That I was now relegated to the back of the bus kids.

The dreams that God put in my heart as a child, were all but dead. I was still serving in my church. I was still praying and reading the Word. I was sharing my faith. But the dream of serving Him full-time in ministry seemed too far to grasp. Out of my reach forever. I had settled for the crumbs that fell from the table.

But over time God began to show me that what happened to me was not meant to destroy me. It did not devalue me. It built me into who I am today. It didn't eliminate me from ministry. It made me more real and vulnerable and opened different avenues of ministry.

A year after my divorce, I was talking with a local

church counselor. They were looking at ways to help singles and newly divorced people. I shared how I really wanted to take a Divorcecare class, but there weren't any classes in my county. So with her prodding, and one year under my belt, I launched a Divorcecare class at a local church – not even my own church! I led two sessions of the course and ministered to over 25 broken and hurting individuals. I trained up leaders who continue to lead the class to this day. This class has been offered over 10 times and ministered to over 100 individuals in their time of brokenness.

As I worked in a law office I developed friendships with my co-workers. Many of my co-workers have been through divorce and loss. I have had many opportunities to share the hope that I had in the midst of the worst days of my life. I remember a co-worker pulling me aside and asking for prayer. She said, "You have had the ****** life I know of and yet you are still happy. I need prayer and I know it works in you."

After two years, I launched a Bible study in my home. I just posted on Facebook asking if anyone was interested. 17 people decided to come each Monday night to my basement to Experience God together. We all grew as we just were real and seeking Him together.

Little by little I had seen God begin to restore my hope that He was not done with me. He placed me in meetings with other ministers who didn't see the invisible scarlet letter I always saw. They saw the God in me. And they pulled it out of me.

I was asked to lead worship ministries at my church when the worship pastor moved away. I wasn't relegated to the back row. I was called to be front and center, worshipping the Lord from a broken and contrite heart. I knew how far He had brought me. I was thankful for every song I was able to lead.

Then I felt the tug to change churches. I was planning to serve on a prayer team once a month. That was my plan. But God had a different vision. Within one month of God planting me at City Point, my pastor and his wife invited me to breakfast and shared God's plan with me. This pastor knew about my divorce. He knew my past. But he only wanted to know my journey with God.

"Do you believe your divorce disqualified you for ministry?" As my pastor's question filled my mind, my eyes began to fill with tears I answered, "I used to think that….. but…. I.. don't… anymore. No." It took a long time to form the words, but with the words came a new level of freedom.

With that realization, I came to learn that the chains I had put on myself because of my divorce were dissolving before my eyes. Where I thought I couldn't do something or be who I was called to be, I began to step into the freedom of Christ. Jesus was not holding me back. He was propelling me forward – fast forward!

I was appointed as a pastor in my church. This is something that would never have happened had I remained married. While I was a minister during my marriage, we were never in churches that would allow women to carry the title of pastor or function in teaching roles.

A whole new world was opening up for me! Suddenly I was getting to serve in ways I had only dreamed of. I wasn't considered less than. I wasn't a director or an assistant to the pastor. I was called a pastor. I was considered an equal, a peer.

I began to recognize that I had a voice. For years I had served, loved, sang and prayed. Now I was able to use my voice to teach, to train, to equip, to impart. Learning to find my voice has been quite an adventure and journey!

For years, I had prayed for our local pastors. Now I am praying with them every single week. These are my colleagues. These are my friends, my brothers and my co-laborers in the Kingdom.

As I mentioned before, I completed my bachelor's degree Suma Cum Laude. I was encouraged along the way. I never thought I would ever go back and complete my degree. No one is too old! God gave me the ability, resources, and time to complete it.

Because of my divorce I found out I had so much more to offer to the Lord. Through the brokenness, He did a work that can only come from suffering. I found HIM in ways I never imagined. He became my everything, because I had nothing. He became my Husband and my Friend that is closer than any brother. He became my Provision and my Provider. He is my Keeper, Deliverer, Healer, and the Lifter of my head.

In the midst of all the amazing doors God was opening, the most surprising gift God gave me was learning who I truly am. I had been married for over twenty years. Most of my life was consumed with being a wife, a mom, a daughter, a prayer leader, a friend. I had known myself by my function or gift. Yet when the titles fell away, I was left to look in a mirror and figure out who was left.

In marriage the two become one. They are not easily torn apart. Yet divorce is all about dividing. The two are separated and part of you becomes lost forever.

In those times I realized how much of me I had lost. I didn't really know who Julie was or even what she liked or wanted. I had been so consumed with living the life I had and surviving that I no longer knew who I was. In my marriage I was one person. My ministry friends would see a different aspect of me. My family would remember the little girl growing up. Yet with time these areas all became separated to the point I did not know who I truly was.

Over time, God began to remind me of who I was and Whose I was. I began to find joy I had missed for years. With the stripping in life came a freedom to be one, whole person. The fragments were removed. The walls had come crumbling down. And I'd rebuild Julie.

Because the most intimate details of my life were very public in my divorce, I realized I had nothing left to hide. The masks were off. And I don't ever want to put them on again. I would not hide what I believed. I would not be afraid to be who God created me to be. I would be authentic, congruent, and real.

Are there masks you are wearing?

Are you wearing the shame of your circumstances?

Do you even know who you are?

Do you long to live a congruent, authentic life?

It is time to break free! You don't have to wear the sin, stigma or shame of the past one day more! There is freedom in Christ. His blood paid the penalty for all our sin. He bore all our shame on the cross. And by the stripes of Jesus Christ we are healed!

You can take the mask the off. Learn who you are. Show the beauty that is within you. See who is hidden beneath the surface. And just BE!!!!

You can trade the garment of shame for the robe of reality. You do not need to wear the stigma, hurt, pain, anger, or betrayal any longer. Shame weighs you down. Take off other's expectations and perceptions of you and learn to walk in the freedom of who Christ created you to be.

You can be whole again! It is possible! It is true!

For over a decade I ran a ministry called Freedom Voices. One of our intercessors would often say to me, "Freedom Voices isn't free, but it will be one day." Over the last few years, I have learned what it means to walk in freedom and have a voice full of the God's freedom. "Whom the Son sets free is free indeed!" There is no turning back.

I do not believe God's best for my life was divorce. Infidelity and abandonment was not His plan. These were sinful choices that carried grave consequences. Yet in the midst of that fiery trial, God was able to produce a purification that would never have happened in either of our lives without these circumstances. God brought gold out of our crucible.

Andy Stanley in his sermon series and book, *Starting Over*, shares how no matter what happened in any broken relationship both parties bear a percentage of responsibility. Whether you were 10% of the problem or 90%, recognize your part in the break down and own it. Confess it to the Lord. Allow His forgiveness to flow freely over you. Partner with the Holy Spirit to bring about the change in your character needed. Then walk FREE!

Friends, what has happened to you and around you is not what qualifies or disqualifies you. It is what God did in you. In the process, I allowed God to mend my heart. He revealed Himself as a forgiving, loving God and showed me how to walk out His character in my everyday life – especially when I didn't feel like it or feel like others deserved it.

He showed me how He can wipe away every tear by bringing healing to my heart and stopping the flow of tears I thought would never end. He brought joy into my life. He allowed me to love again and to live again. He brought the oil of joy for my mourning.

He put a new song in my mouth and a new step in my feet. He has led me down paths I could have never dreamed of. He has given me grace for each and every day. I can only stand back and say, "WOW GOD!" when I think of what the Lord has done.

When the devastation happened, I never dreamed I would get to do what I do today. I never dreamed I'd write this book. I never dreamed of being on staff at a church. I never dreamed of living again. I never dreamed of loving again. God is good and faithful.

"I waited patiently for the LORD; and He inclined to

*me, and heard my cry. He also brought me up out
of a horrible pit, out of the miry clay, and set my
feet upon a rock, and established my steps. He has
put a new song in my mouth – praise to our God;
many will see it and fear and will trust in the Lord."*
Psalm 40:1-3

No matter how horrible the pit, God has a rope of
hope to pull you out! In the words of Corrie ten
Boom, a Holocaust survivor, " No pit is so deep that
He is not deeper still, with Jesus even in our
darkest moments, the best remains and the very
best is yet to be."

God can use ANYTHING surrendered to Him.
However, in the surrender we let go of our agendas
and plans. We pick up His. We have to allow Him
to reveal Himself in the midst of the heart ache and
hurt, the pain and the pressures, the
disappointment and the discouragement. And
when He reveals His power and presence, there is
nothing that remains the same!

I am not the same girl I was when my ex-husband
left. I can't be. You will not be the same either.
You get to choose if the situation you walked
through will make you better or bitter. There are
only two options in hurt – better or bitter.

Which is it?

What do YOU choose?

"Choose for yourselves this day whom you will serve…." Joshua 24:15

We each have a choice and our choices have consequences. We each can make our choice, but we don't get to determine the consequences. The choices you make are setting the trajectory of your life.

Where you choose to focus will determine your final outcome. If you choose to focus on God, His faithfulness and the new opportunities He puts before you, you can grow and become even better. But if you focus only on the hurt and heart ache, you will grow cold and bitter. You will choose to wall yourself off from everyone who could help you or love you. If you allow a root of bitterness to grow in your heart, you will become bitter. Hebrews 12: 15 teaches us that our bitterness will defile many. It is like poison to us and to those around us. We will infect many with our bitterness.

Your decision will impact not only you but also your family and those following you. *"I call heaven and earth as witnesses today against you, that I have set before you life and death, blessing and cursing; therefore choose life, that both you and your descendants may live. "* Deuteronomy 30:10

Have you ever noticed that person who was hurt 20 years ago but still is bitter? It is etched on their faces. The painful venom is still coming out of their mouths. They are frozen in time , locked to the hurt or offense that occurred.

Our bitterness will harden our heart. Our relationship with the Lord will grow cold. We will not have the communion we could have with Him or others until we repent and remove this root from our hearts. Bitterness and unforgiveness will be like a slow terminal illness to our emotional and spiritual life, causing death along its path.

Forgiveness opens the pathway for healing and life. John 10:10 states that Jesus came to give us abundant life. God is still writing your story! This brokenness can be just a chapter, not a conclusion, to your book of life.

Don't allow this to be the end. See the challenges as doorways that you will walk through. Each door leads to a new broader place. A place of freedom, hope, and love. You get the opportunity to change and grow through the process.

John Bevere writes in the book, *The Bait of Satan*, "If you stay free from offense you will stay in God's will. If you become offended, you will be taken captive by the enemy to fulfill his own purpose and will. Take your pick. It is much more beneficial to stay free from offense…..often the thing that looks like an abortion of God's plan actually ends up being the road to its fulfillment if we stay in obedience and free from offense."

Most of us do not like change. We are extremely change resistant. Until the pain of staying the same is greater than the pain involved with changing, we typically do not change. In divorce, our lives are thrown into change - whether we like it or not. Nothing can remain the same.

In that forced change, growth can occur. We can grow in ways we never dreamed. We will try things we might never have done before.

You have heard my story. You have seen how God has brought about amazing opportunities from the depths of my destruction. God breathed new life into dreams I thought had died.

What are the dreams you never thought you would accomplish? What is holding you back? Where do you need God to breathe new life?

God is setting before you open doors. You get to run through them. A new destiny awaits you. I heard a pastor share, "Your disappointments lead to God's reappointment." I have seen God shift and move me into so many new areas. I have been able to do things I never would have dreamed before.

Revelation 21:5 states that God makes all things new. It is time to step into the new that He has for you. The old ways are gone and cannot be reborn as they were. But each day we are given the opportunity for the new of God to come forth.

Determine to seek the Lord. Allow Him to place a new dream within you. Imagine the good that He has in store.

What have you always wished you could do? What is holding you back? Make an action plan and take a step. Forward progress is made one step at a time.

For years I knew I would write this book to help others on their journey. However, when I was just thinking about it, nothing happened. However, as I determined to write each day for a short period of time, this book came together.

It is the same with any area of our life. Sustainable progress usually doesn't appear with huge leaps, but much is accomplished in the faithful steps. Day in, day out. One step after another step after another step.

Do you want to start a business? Write your business plan. Interview other business leaders. Get training. Launch small and watch it grow.

Want to improve your emotional health? Schedule an appointment with a counselor. Go and grow!

Want to improve your health? Start exercising daily. Change your daily eating habits. It doesn't happen overnight. It happens day by day by day of consistent obedience to your plan.

God also has a plan for you! His plan is to prosper

you and give you a future and a hope! Take time to get His plan. Dream together with Him and then implement it.

Your best is yet to come! Believe Him! Dream! Live!

Hold nothing back.

God is faithful.

He is your Keeper.

JULIE HAYDEN

ABOUT THE AUTHOR

Julie Hayden is a kept woman! She has witnessed the goodness of God and freely shares of the hope that He has given her. She is a mom to two grown sons and loves the life God has given her. Julie serves as a pastor at City Point Church in Portage, Indiana. She has committed the last two decades of her life to seeing the Body of Christ in Northwest Indiana unite together in prayer. God has used her to build bridges between churches and tear down dividing walls establishing His will on the earth as it is in heaven. She is a songwriter and has published two additional books:
Reset & A Daughter's Diary.

For more information, visit her blog
adventuresinhopeblog.wordpress.com

Made in the USA
Middletown, DE
23 February 2022

61643828R00050